CREATIVE GENIUS

The Inspirational Wisdom of Pen Women

Edited by
Kathleen Powers-Vermaelen

Creative Genius:
The Inspirational Wisdom of Pen Women

Cover art and design by Lucy Arnold
Golden Gate-Marin County Branch
www.lucyarnold.com

ISBN 13: 978-0-9815693-8-3

Published by
PEN WOMEN PRESS
1300 17th Street, NW
Washington, DC 20036-1901

Founded in 1897, the National League of American Pen Women,
Inc., is a non-profit dedicated to promoting the arts.
Visit our web site and blog at www.nlapw.org.

Printed in the United States of America.

First edition

Editor's Forward:

What you now hold in your hands, dear reader, began as an NLAPW blog series that published semi-regularly on Fridays from February until October of 2017. By the time "the Creative series" had completed, I knew that I'd curated something unique—an original anthology of feminine wit, wisdom and willpower that deserved a permanent home in print.

Creative Genius: The Inspirational Wisdom of Pen Women teems with sage advice from women who have mastered their art and become experts in their craft. Herein, readers will learn what inspires the artist and drives her creative process, how she sets up an effective workspace and navigates business/legal requirements, and why women continue to create despite the professional and personal challenges that befall them.

I thank my wonderful authors—all fellow Pen Women—who gave their time and talent to this project: Dorothy Atkins, Dr. Patricia Daly-Lipe, Sara Etgen-Baker, Lois Batchelor Howard, Kathryn Kleekamp, Carol S. Mann, Elizabeth Diane Garcia Martin, Mary Joan Meagher, Sheila Meyerowitz-Firestone, Ronni Miller, Linda A. Mohr, Bobbie Dumas Panek, Marsha J. Perlman, Tricia Pimental, Sarah Byrn Rickman, Bonnie Jo Smith, Connie Spittler, Rodika Tollefson, Katie Turner, Laura Walth, and Janis Ward. I am also grateful to Lucy Arnold for agreeing to design our beautiful book covers. Without these ladies' dedication and willingness to answer the call, this book never would have been possible.

May the advice and acumen shared within the following pages inspire all to create prolifically, proudly, and often!

Kathleen Powers-Vermaelen
Managing Editor, Pen Women Press
Publications Chair, 2016-2018
NLAPW, Inc.

TABLE OF CONTENTS

PART ONE:

Creative Inspiration

FROM WHERE OR WHAT DO YOU DRAW INSPIRATION?

Lois Batchelor Howard
Palm Springs Branch
poetlois1@outlook.com

I am blessed or cursed. I don't know which. Perhaps both. If I describe my living on a farm, that will possibly explain why or how I write. I'll give it a go.

Every time I look behind the house or the barn, for that matter, I see them there or I see them coming. Actually, they've been coming for a long time. They're odd things: sometimes strange, always different, fascinating somehow. They're always there, it seems. Grandma Bryce might have called them "wonderful pains," like she described the aches in her legs that would not go away.

They have me caught; I know that.

When I've had the courage, I've asked my neighbors. Funny... they don't see them, and they give me looks like I give a field of corn that, for no reason I can figure out, has suddenly stopped growing. Or is it the look I feel when it's harvest time and the combine has broken down? Maybe it's more like I'm asking 'em to an opera and they know that I know, more than the smell of bundled hay in the early dew of dawn, that they love country music. Whatever. I can't pinpoint the look, but I've felt it before; it's not a stranger to me. It's kind of "puttin' up with," and it unsettles me some, but not enough to stop seeing those things.

They sit atop the trees on the horizon by Nelson Rathbun's place, and they often shoot right out of the setting sun or the rising sun. I see lots of both, but there are more chores in the mornings. They ride the backs of cows. Sometimes they get the

8

chickens clucking and squawking, and the hogs squalling and the dogs barking, runnin' around in frenzied circles, the horses bolting their heads sideways, restlessly shifting their weight back and forth in closed stalls.

Yes, these things have found me. They are powerful things, I tell you. I know I said it before, but it seems they are always here. Sometimes they're in my boots when I go to put 'em on in the morning or they stick to my high-tops after a heavy rain, when I've had to gluck trough-deep in mud. At times, they even leap out in the black of night. They're here, all right, and—how does the expression go? *They must have seen me coming!* Or I, them.

I could use a lot of fancy words, maybe. Straight of it is, we get along. Oh, sometimes I put 'em off, but mostly I grin and welcome them in. You don't get that much company with all this land around and the houses so far apart. I don't even always treat them to electricity; sometimes I light an old oil lamp and over the oilcloth table cover, shadows visiting on the walls, we sit down together. I rustle up some hot tea and biscuits and blank papers, set the ink jar down, and dip my quill into the ink that somehow reminds me of the clear spring water trickling down near the pond at the top of the hill. But I'm getting' off the subject, in a way, and I'm repeatin' myself. I tend to do that. My listeners keep reminding me that I do, but you *do what ya gotta do.*

"Friend-Things," I say, "What poems do you have for me today?" As they keep prattling on, which is our way when we're together, I write. Oh, sometimes we take a break and check the larder or the root cellar. They tell me that's why they come, and sometimes we gaze out over the acres and know there's a lot of promise in that old Spring earth, buds of words and greens sproutin' up all over... Why, those things are there now, out there again, dancin', like they own the place.

They've been lookin' over my shoulder, and they say they like readin', that I draw inspiration from livin' here on the farm and listenin' to them. Gotta give credit where credit is due.

MUSINGS OF A STRUGGLING NOVELIST

Sara Etgen-Baker
Dallas Branch
sab_1529@yahoo.com

When I began writing in 2010, I was especially comfortable and adept in writing memoirs about the people of my childhood and early adult years in my native Texas. I became known for my ability to connect with readers by giving them authentic, familiar characters, a sensitive narrator, and a keen sense of place—but in 2014, I turned to fiction writing and began the rather daunting task of writing my first novel.

I was the first to admit that I knew little about writing fiction or writing something as major as a novel, but I had an idea birthed from a real-life family situation. So, I began and painstakingly put words on pages, hoping to create convincing characters, scenes with emotional value, and a believable storyline that would engage and captivate readers. Oh, how I labored over my characters and scenes!

The months passed. Words slowly became pages, and pages became chapters. By December 2016, I was deeply into writing Chapter 15 of approximately 20 chapters. When the new year arrived, however, I became increasingly dissatisfied with my story and disillusioned with my ability to complete my novel. Honestly, I simply wasn't motivated.

I'm not a quitter, though, and flatly refused to give up on a project begun so humbly years ago. I began losing sleep and often laid awake at night thinking about my characters—their strengths, their flaws, and their humanity. During the early morning hours, I played with the story line, scenes, plots, and subplots. With the lack of sleep, I became even more muddled and confused.

January gave way to February. Sunless, harsh days prevailed; winter's blue dreariness settled over me, further stifling my creativity. March arrived, bringing the warmth of the sun's rays, but I was still unable to write.

Last week, I sat down at my desk with the sole task of making some sense of my collection of notes and putting some order to my rather haphazardly organized files. I hoped that task would ground me, but alas, it only served to further muddy the novel-writing waters.

So, I took to power walking a couple of hours a day hoping that the fresh air and open space would broaden my horizon and give me perspective. At this point, I'm quite certain my neighbors, amazed as they are with my persistence and dedication, questioned why I walked for so long.

Then, I took to pruning flowers in our garden, pulling weeds (symbolic? yes), and working myself to the point of exhaustion, believing that exhaustion would surely help me sleep. Still, sleep alluded me. Something about my novel was haunting me—but what was it?

Then I had an epiphany of sorts. I am a vastly different person now than I was when I began writing my novel, yet I was trying to write and create from my old perspective. My characters had become unauthentic, and my scenes evoked no emotions—they were ineffective, extraneous, and disconnected from the overall story line. Every word I'd written seemed flat.

So, in desperation, I re-read my synopsis and each of my completed chapters. Then came the stark realization that so many novelists face: This was my "shitty" first draft. No doubt about it. What I'd written thus far wasn't that good at all. Disappointment and mild panic set in. For the first time since I began writing, I feared beginning again.

Before opening my laptop to begin anew, I literally marked through anything that didn't enrich the story, eliminating so many words, paragraphs, pages, and even entire scenes and chapters. Now, I was left with only about six good chapters, and I had huge gaps in my story line and in my character development.

Ah, where to go from here? I shall begin at the beginning and start anew, knowing that I've not failed at novel writing. On the contrary, I've been tremendously successful and gutsy. I've been on a learning curve—and a huge one at that!

The most important lesson I've learned is this: To grow as a person, I had to let go of old truths, old thinking, and old habits. I had to relinquish my control of expectations and outcomes and allow my life to unfold naturally.

To grow as a writer, I must let go of old words and unproductive writing habits. I need to relinquish my control of a specific outcome and then let my story unfold, for it's in the unfolding that my story will develop naturally. It's in my letting go where the heart of both life and story lie and where creativity truly dwells.

I returned to my laptop, opened it, clicked on Microsoft Word, and began a new chapter in my writing life. And, yes, I'm exhausted—but oddly, I'm refreshed.

I bet I'll sleep better tonight!

FROM LULLABIES TO GAP YEARS

Sheila Meyerowitz-Firestone
Boca Raton Branch
sheilafirestone.com

From the days of their births to the daily conversations, I do not know exactly when or how the new composition ideas will arrive, but they do. Staring at Lital's birth picture, in the Sylvester Cancer Center doctors' waiting room, the words and melody for "I've Stamped your Picture on my Heart," arrives. This song later becomes part of a curriculum and series of songs, a *Songs for a New Day* program called *Sing and Think*.

From photos of little girls growing up in Northern, Israel, to "Welcome Little Wonder" (a song for Emily), "Berceuse" for Noah, and lullabies for Maya and Allie, six grandchildren have become my sources of inspiration. The oldest, now 22, is on a fellowship in another country. Three others recently had their first work experiences. Their challenges often become my musical challenges, works derived from the joy of savoring who they are, what they face, what their delights are, and how each meet and greets the day. A recent event in Charlottesville, Virginia, where the oldest received her master's degree and taught, another's struggles to achieve excellence on the job, other internships, and gap years with studies abroad have all become part of my musical collections.

Works are begun by nothing more than a touch, a photo, a Facebook moment, a tug of the heart, a tear, a smile, a skip and a *Hi, Grandma. How are you?* text message. I hear this story repeated by many grandparents. We tell the stories and paint their moments in our works. We are filled with the joy of expectation and the hope that our grandchildren's lives will impact the world.

Berceuse

For Noah Jordan Firestone

Sheila Firestone

Piano

Lital's third birthday present brings "The Peace Patch" dance suite and curriculum. The premiere was planned for our visit to the Israeli "Gan" preschool. "The Grandchildren's Suite," piano anthology, commemorates the budding interests of the six, as does the arrival of "The Cat Sarah," who plays *Kitten on the Keys* quite well.

"Miriam and the Women of the Desert," a musical/operetta, includes several lullabies originally written for the grandchildren. "Peace Child," was created for Allie's birth. I use it in the Miriam work to depict Mother Yocheved singing her hopes to the baby Moses. Batya, his Egyptian mother, sings "In the Cradle of Mankind." The opening Prologue begins with the search for God. It calls chorally on a number of modern Hebrew names given to God. It was inspired by a small child's private conversation with God outside.

An internship or a first job with challenges becomes a sonata or symphony. These are my tributes to youth and my hopes for their success. I am grateful that the ideas translate into musical ideas to play with when I am not with these young people as they continue on their paths. So, thank you, dear grandchildren, for a lifetime of inspiration. I am always with you, continuing to be filled with wonder by your actions. May you always find joy as you use your energies to fulfill your dreams.

Berceuse sheet music image, page 14, supplied by Sheila Meyerowitz-Firestone

SEARCHING FOR LIFE

Janis Ward
Fort Lauderdale Branch

Birds have always been my passion since childhood. Our small yellow canary entertained us with cheery chirps from his cage in our kitchen and delighted us as he made his swing go back and forth. As a teen, I acquired a beautiful, brightly-colored parakeet who used to sit on the edges of our coffee cups and fly into the dining room mirror to join the "other bird" there.

My husband and boys often went duck hunting, returning home with those beautiful birds for me to cook. It almost broke my heart. We also raised ducks from babies in our atrium pond and garden. It was fascinating to watch them grow. One day, a neighborhood boy brought us an owl that had been hit by a car, which we nursed back to health and watched fly away to freedom with great joy.

We winter now in Florida, as do the birds. When we first drive into the golf course-condo area in Pompano Beach, we are fascinated by the activity on a small lake. Ibis, a few pelicans, and occasionally one or two storks wander freely on the grass lawn. Many are diving and swimming in the water. Often there are so many, they block the cars. Most drivers slow down to avoid the beautiful white birds.

Having been an artist since childhood, I often paint birds. There is nothing more thrilling than a flock of 200 or so squawking parakeets following their leader, bunched together. Geese are interesting to watch as well.

I came upon a large white swan who'd lost his mate a few years ago. They mate for life, so it was hurtful to see him always swimming alone in his large wooded pond. What a delight, however, to find a large black Anhinga stretching his wings to dry and hanging around with this gorgeous swan.

The winter of 2016 in Florida brought some disastrous news to birding lovers. The flocks of ibis were nearly nonexistent. I kept looking for them and wondering why they weren't in their pond. Finally, a newspaper article explained it all: Because of the ocean's rising, salt water has infiltrated the pond, killing the small fish on which the large ibis had been feeding. Where the ibis went, I don't know, but they are missed.

And so, I continue to paint these beautiful creatures in their winter habitat. A watercolor I painted in early 2017 shows the ibis wandering among the shrubs, looking for food. It is entitled "Searching for Life." Whether the birds can survive on worms and such is a big question. I'm certain many more paintings will come as I follow their plight.

MY PARKINSON'S MUSE

Linda A. Mohr
Boca Raton Branch
lindamohr.com

I was like a graduate student researching primary sources. The starting point was the end—my poetry collection to uncover what inspires me. As I reviewed content, the answer slid into nature, objects and grief categories.

I started writing poetry in 2013 after attending a haiku lecture at the North Palm Beach Library. The myriad of sensory delights while vacationing at the Missouri family farm inspired me to create over fifty haiku poems in two weeks. Bobwhite, amber wheat, alfalfa bale, honeysuckle, cocklebur, sweet pea tendrils and tasseled corn images, along with chirp, chatter, squawk, screech and meow sounds, found poetic expression. My first prose poem, "The Rocking Chair," was created on the same trip in response to an empty lawn chair swaying to and fro. I imagined my spiritual mother visiting her homestead, and we were rocking side by side in conversation. *The companion chair sits vacant. Or does it?*

During this time frame, I was diagnosed with Parkinson's. A fascinating twist of this progressive neurological movement disorder is creativity. Research studies find some patients suddenly begin a new art pursuit such as painting or sculpting or become more prolific in writing books. Although I published a memoir in 2008 and maintained a blog, poetry was not in my toolbox. Perhaps it was coincidental, but without formal education in poetry, I simply wrote about what touched my heart.

Intrigued by how my mother's medical alert system talked to her in response to buttons being pushed, I wrote "The Magic Button" poem. More than anything I wanted the machine to answer my question. *My mother is in heaven. I want to talk to her. What button do I push?*

On an autumn trip to Lake Toxaway in North Carolina, my cabin was surrounded by trees showing and shedding their beauty. As I sat on the deck and watched leaves in various shapes and sizes falling in different ways, the leaves reminded me of people. Later I spread the dried reminders out on a table and created "Fallen Leaves, Fallen Lives" poem. *Doubled over leaf drops, Mottled and worn out.*

After the devastating loss of my beloved Maine Coon, I penned my "Morning Visitor" poem. She had a unique way of communicating (google "Lexie Lee's Meowlogue") in life, so I was certain she would send me a message in spirit. She did not disappoint! *Unexplained lightness on bed. Spot where you use to snuggle.*

The most astounding outpouring of poetry occurred when I was on a long flight to Portland, Oregon, in 2016 to attend a Parkinson's Congress. Fourteen poems on loss, death and grief relating to my boyfriend's passing twenty-seven years ago were created. *Two by two they came. Carrying food trays.*

Although more study is needed on Parkinson's and creativity, I am grateful for whatever force drives me to write poetry. The results of creating over fifty prose poems in four years, winning awards, being published, and studying under presidential inaugural poet Richard Blanco bring a smile to my masked Parkinson's face.

SEASON TO SEASON

Sara Etgen-Baker
Dallas Branch
sab_1529@yahoo.com

When the alarm sounded, I wanted to continue sleeping. Instead, I slid out of the warm sheets away from the comfort of my husband's body, peeked through the Venetian blinds, and noticed graceful flakes of pearly-white lace had dusted the tree-lined trails adjacent to my home. Even though the mercury hovered just below freezing, I knew today was the perfect day for a solitary winter run. So, I quietly donned my winter running clothes and headed downstairs.

Daylight had not yet turned the slumberous, dark blue clouds to their morning gray, and—for a moment—I hesitated at my front door not wanting to disturb winter's peaceful silence. When I stepped outside, my warm breath mingled with the crisp, cold air as it stung my cheeks. As I began to run, my stiff legs begged me to turn around; I ignored their cries knowing they would soon stop complaining. Only my footfalls broke the silence as the gentle snow crunched under my feet.

As I ran through the woods that morning, nary an animal crossed my path; their tracks in the snow indicated that they had been here before me, though. The nippy air frosted my breath, and soon my breathing mixed with my footfalls creating a rhythm. I ran effortlessly past fallen trees along the creek side with no thought of time or distance. I wasn't aware of speed either—just movement.

I ran past an icy pond cloaked by barren, frost-covered trees trembling like skeletons in the brisk wind. Snow began falling around me, making me feel as if I was running in a snow globe. Soon, winter's tranquility and purity enveloped me; time and distance became meaningless, and I imagined that the woods looked as it once did 100 years ago. I gazed into the distance and, for a moment, I thought I saw Henry David Thoreau standing outside his cabin near Walden Pond. He was not there, of course; there was no one and nothing except for what was right in front of me—miles of glorious solitude.

For years I've run alone along these trails in the woods—a quiet, almost sacred place every bit as wondrous as Walden Pond. Generally, the only sounds I hear on these solitary runs are birds chirping; small animals collecting nuts; and my feet as they gently land on leaves, pine straws, or snow. I occasionally hear the pitter-patter of rain drops as they hit leaves and fall onto the underbrush and forest floor. Sometimes a light rain cools my perspiring body and soothes my spirit. Frequently, I immerse myself in my thoughts and dreams, and I feel invigorated. Other times, the solitude nourishes the seeds of stories germinating in my head.

Here in the woods, though, solitude—as silent and powerful as light itself—forces introspection. So, I linger in the solitude emptying and quieting my mind; then, I let go of the world and my ego—journeying inwards. Here, I sometimes hear my inner voice whispering to me; I occasionally meet myself face-to-face and find the being within—the *true self*—that has been waiting patiently to be discovered. I continue running, grateful for the solitude and the balance I now feel. At some point, I must turn around, follow my footprints, and return in the direction from whence I came. Reluctantly, I approach the end of my solitary run, not wanting it to be over.

From season to season, I've run alone along the quiet trails in the nearby woods, and I've taken great pleasure in the solitude it offers. To quote Thoreau, "I have an immense appetite for solitude, like an infant for sleep." I discovered long ago that solitude is necessary for me, for that's where my creativity dwells. I can no more live without creativity than I can live without sleep.

PART TWO:
Creative Advice

SHINE YOUR LIGHT

Mary Joan Meagher
Minnesota Branch
maryjoanmeagher@gmail.com

From time to time, writers are caught in darkness. Shadows obscure choices and chase one down hallways of doubt. A writer sits at her computer and feels blocked, lacking in vision, miserable. How best to find the light and how best to flee the darkness becomes her quest.

Those of us who live in Minnesota and other northern states are very familiar with the experience of living in darkness. During the winter months, our days are shortened day by day, and sunlight retreats to the South, angling itself lower and lower on the horizon. Clouds cover the sky in November, hiding the rim of the sun in gray tatters, bringing cold rain, damp wind, and then the snows of winter.

But look at the artists in our midst who paint with light for films and television. They bring us laughter and joy. Look at the rainbow itself, the spectrum of light arched across the sky, shattering the darkness of the storm that has preceded it by crystallizing the raindrops into prisms. We see light refracted into all its colors, promising hope and happiness to all.

Writing our truths is one way to bring this light to others. Perhaps at one time or another one may be in the pits or lost in the blues. We need someone or something to lead us out.

Writing in a personal journal is always therapeutic. Write your truth freely, sorting out your feelings, examining your perceptions of time, place, and life events. Getting your thoughts and feelings on paper is the best way to unblock your creativity. Reaching out to others, asking for help, and finding a listening ear brings us grace and light to share with others. Once we have been gifted with this light or these insights into life, we too can spread it to those in need.

The psychologist Carl Gustav Jung says, "As far as we can discern, the sole purpose of human existence is to kindle a light in the darkness of mere being." It is up to each of us to kindle this light for all those who are part of our daily lives.

Life is light, and warmth, and love. We all have plentiful supply of those qualities. Make each twenty-four hours a gift to your associates by living each day with truth, sympathy, and unconditional love, by unblocking your creativity, and by writing the truths you have discovered, passing them on to your readers. Just as you turn your face to the sun to soak up its rays, so turn your face to others to give them the gift of your light. In the dark days of winter, you can bring the light of spring to those who surround you.

As an old African-American spiritual says, "*This little light of mine, I'm gonna let it shine/This little light of mine, I'm gonna let it shine/Let it shine, let it shine, let it shine!*"

ARRANGING A PERSONAL WORKSPACE ZONE

Tricia Pimental
Bayou City II Branch
www.triciapimental.com

As far as creative inspirational wisdom goes, what follows are a few thoughts on arranging a personal work zone. *Writer's Digest* editor and author Elizabeth Sims gives plenty of useful tips in her book, *You've Got a Book in You*. They've helped me, and perhaps they will do the same for you.

Sims refers to the place where we hopefully will get our brains into gear as our "garret." Two factors to consider when creating a garret are: 1. it's a frame of mind, as in "Nothing and no one can distract me from writing," and 2. it must have usable work space.

A room in your house is nice, but family members will still sense your presence. They'll feel free to knock on the door, or worse, barge in while you are in the middle of constructing a clever metaphor or the most brilliant plot line ever conceived.

If you're lucky enough to have access to a real garret—a cozy attic space—try that out. You'll probably have a window and literally feel "above it all." Barring that, a corner in your local library or favorite coffee shop might do nicely. Even part of your garage, provided it's heated and well-lit, could work. Avoid basements if possible, as they can be dark, musty, or chilly.

Here are seven tips to help you shape it into the perfect place of inspiration:

1. Find a suitable work surface

Whether it's a table, desk, or counter, something solid is required. Your lap is for children and cats, puppies and pillows, and your laptop—but only for brief periods of time. Checking your email? Fine. Writing a key chapter in your mystery? Probably not.

2. Sit in a comfortable chair

Sounds obvious, right? But there's more to it. What's your mindset? An office chair that swivels, has armrests, and good back support can make you feel official and in charge of your writing session. Maybe you are more at home in the efficiency of a straight back chair. Are you having trouble committing to getting something on the page? Maybe the temporary nature of a stool will help you dip your toe into the literary water. Whatever you choose, make sure you have an ergonomic match to your writing surface.

3. Clear the clutter

Even if you subscribe to the "messy desk is the sign of genius" philosophy, your mind will be clearer if distractions are at a minimum. *The Life-Changing Magic of Tidying Up* by Marie Kondo helped me enormously. You'll never look at "stuff" the same way again.

4. Keep things within reach

My cell phone sits in a stand on a section of my L-shaped arrangement because I don't want to hunt for it when it rings (assuming I haven't turned it off). I also have three baskets at hand: one for notes on works in progress, another for electronic accessories like extra chargers, cables, and, because I live overseas, adaptors. The third is for vitamins, protein bars, and yes, chocolate.

5. Light up your life

Remember Tom Hanks in the opening scene of *Joe versus the Volcano*? Forego fluorescence and use full-spectrum light bulbs that emulate the sun. You'll feel happier and more energetic.

Similarly, because extended time in front of the computer screen is taxing, consider investing in a pair of tinted glasses designed to reduce eyestrain.

6. Bring on nature

Fresh flowers rejuvenate your space. The colors of yellow and orange are especially effective in stimulating the senses. Plants help counteract the energy drain from electronics like your desktop or printer. I opted for orchids, enjoying both living greens and colorful blooms in one unit.

7. Sights and sounds

First, sights: Open the windows, not just for fresh air, but to get inspired. I have a view of the Mafra National Palace from my office at home. It always transports me. Have you won writing, speaking, or other recognition? Put these on display on your wall or book shelf. Remind yourself that you *have been*, *are*, and *will be* an achiever. Don't have any awards yet? Set a goal to get one.

As for sound, this choice is so personal, there is no rule. I have trouble with background music because I start remembering when and where I first heard a song. It's the worst with oldies. But I have the TV—news, movie, whatever—on almost all the time. I feel like I'm missing something otherwise. I think I'm in the minority on this one and would love to hear what you think about it.

I hope these suggestions will help you construct a new, or improve an existing, creative zone. If your area is public—a corner in your local library or "coffee-ing hole"—then your control over that space is obviously more limited than if you have a dedicated space in your home. Either way, you can do a lot to facilitate your process.

SO, YOUR BOOK IS FINALLY PUBLISHED... NOW WHAT?

Kathryn Kleekamp
Cape Cod Branch
www.SandwichArt.com

Whether your book is published by a major publisher or self-published, your masterpiece will sit in its carton unless it's actively promoted. Although my publisher (Schiffer) lists my book in its catalog and distributes it to Amazon and traditional book stores, I've found the tips I offer below essential to boost sales. Many authors and artists either shy away from or dislike marketing, but believe me, it will grow on you. As an author and artist, I've met many delightful people at signings and book talks. If a piece of art or a book subject resonates with the viewer or reader, it makes for an instant connection between two strangers.

In my case, casual meetings with those who have purchased my work have led to some satisfying, long-term relationships. At a marketing seminar I once attended, the very successful speaker said that most of one's sales will come from repeat customers. For me, it's been true. After purchasing a book or artwork for themselves, many have come back time and again to purchase gifts for others.

Here are eight suggestions for ways to promote your book and increase sales:

1. **Visit local book stores, gift shops and museums to arrange signings**. Establish yourself as a real person, not just a title. It makes a world of difference.

2. **Create a simple website and Facebook Page**. You can offer useful tidbits from your book without openly

proclaiming, "Please buy my book." Post things that are insightful or helpful to the reader.

3. **Approach your local community television and radio stations to arrange an interview.** Be prepared to give them a book beforehand. If they interview you, post the video on your website.

4. **Depending on the topic of your book, contact regional book clubs, women's clubs, libraries, churches, retirement communities, Newcomers clubs, senior centers etc., to arrange a book talk.** It's important to assess your audience beforehand and narrow your comments to things they would be most interested in. Keep your presentation fresh for yourself as well as your listeners.

5. **Send a query letter or story idea to local newspapers and magazines to see if they will write a human-interest story about you and your book.** News organizations are always looking for fresh material to print. It's important to indicate why your story is of interest to their readers. What sets you and your book apart from all others?

6. **Do a little research to find out who local media book reviewers are.** Send them a copy of your book with a cover letter to see if they would be willing to write a review. As you accumulate reviews, even if they're from a friend or colleague, print a list to display wherever you have a talk or show.

7. **Many communities have outdoor summer fairs or holiday bazaars.** The cost to rent table space is small and usually there are large crowds.

8. **To make point of purchase sales, the Square app for your cell phone is a wonderful way to process credit card sales.** There is no monthly fee and a very small processing fee. Many purchases are impulsive; you don't want to miss out on buyers who may not have cash.

SIX STEPS FOR DEALING WITH REJECTIONS

Kathleen Powers-Vermaelen
Member-at-Large
kathleenpowersvermaelen.blogspot.com

The worst rejection letter I ever received came from a small Colorado-based "literary" magazine that billed itself as prime literature for the doctor's office waiting room.

I'm going to let the above line stand alone and sink in. Consider for a moment, if you will, the plight of the writer. Good writing doesn't just happen; it takes time and effort. Querying literary magazines to get the writing published, thereby validating said expended time and effort, takes even more time and effort. The higher profile publications receive hundreds, perhaps thousands, of stories each month. Competition for placement is fierce, and refusals are many.

Rejection-free indie publishing has removed some of the sting, but even these authors will admit they'd rather have someone accept and publish their work "traditionally," which is the only reason why we continue to subject ourselves to the often soul-crushing process of querying.

This, of course, brings me back to my opening sentence. The rejecting publication was not *The Paris Review*. It was something people read while waiting to get their tonsils swabbed for a strep test. Moreover, it was spreading streptococcal bacteria to the next unsuspecting reader/patient, and then to the one after that.

What I'm trying to say here, gently, is that I wasn't aiming all that high.

Even so, I'd done my homework by reading the publication and developing a feel for what the editors liked. I selected a story that fit their style. After drafting a professional query letter, I mailed out the still-warm manuscript out first class. For a few days, I basked in the pleasant possibility that another one of my stories would be published.

Less than a week later, a S.A.S.E. arrived in my mailbox. At once, I knew that a single sheet of paper was inside—never a good sign.

Sighing, I tore it open, expecting the usual: *Thank you for your submission. Unfortunately, we do not feel it is right for our publication. We wish you the best of luck placing it elsewhere.* These form rejection letters are unsigned and grainy from years of having been photocopied off other yellowing photocopies of the first form rejection letter ever written, no doubt penned and printed by Gutenberg himself. Like most professional writers, I've received more than my fair share of them.

What I found inside, however, was something altogether different. In my hands was the same query letter I'd mailed out only days earlier. Right underneath my signature, the editor had written in two-inch-tall block letters with a red Sharpie marker:

NO!

It's difficult to describe what went through my mind and in what order. I remember an initial flash of mortification, looking around to see if someone was filming my reaction for an updated Candid Camera series, and finally, righteous indignation. Would it have killed the editor to have been polite? After all, he'd solicited submissions in *Novel & Short Story Writer's Market*. Why respond like I'd shown up selling vacuum cleaners door-to-door just as dinner was being put on the table?

Rejection sucks in general, but it especially blows when delivered by sucker-punch from a decidedly mediocre publication. My good friend Erin, a talented poet, shared her own frustration when her work was rejected by another "literary" magazine that was—I kid you not—printed on typing paper and then crookedly stapled with such amateurish aplomb that it made me, a former print production manager for a Fortune 500 company, want to throw its editors into a cage and spray them with a fire hose until they screamed for mercy. At least they'd had the decency, however, to be polite to her.

This is where I (hopefully) impart some inspirational wisdom as a takeaway from this mock-horror story. Another good friend and connoisseur of ironic meditations, Tim, posted a meme on Facebook a few months ago containing a variation of the Latin phrase "*Illegitimi non carborundum.*" Loosely translated, it advises not letting those not-so-nice folks succeed in discouraging one's efforts—good advice, even if stated in a somewhat mysterious and indelicate way. (Google the phrase for the actual translation, but not in the company of those with fragile sensibilities.)

Here are some practical steps to take with your own rejection letters, based on my ample experience:

1. Read them.
2. If they say something useful, consider the advice. Such feedback is rare!
3. If they *don't* say something useful, shred them.
4. Better yet, line a cage with them and allow a bird to "critique" them.
5. Or ceremoniously burn them, if you're into that kind of thing.
6. Then, for the love of all that's creative, *move on*! That's what I did.

Illegitimi non carborundum, folks. Keep on creating!

THE WRITTEN WORDS OF WOMEN

Connie Spittler
Omaha Branch
conkspittler@live.com

The poet Muriel Rukeyser asked, "What would happen if one woman told the truth about her life?" Her answer: "The world would split open."

We hold a universal knowledge within us. Telling it, sharing it, writing it down sets the commotion in motion. Like a breakfast egg, we crack open the sphere that is our world and find our truth, the simple wisdom that comes from our life stories.

We belong to an ancient tribe of storytellers, a long line of ancestors who washed clothes down by the river and remembered, who sewed at quilting bees and talked of the past, who cooked for harvesters and shared stories, who held children on warm laps and whispered true tales. Today, in shopping malls and beauty shops, on cell phones and during coffee breaks, women talk of life's unfolding events. No matter where it happens, this is storytelling, one of our oldest traditions. Our stories become a lasting tribute to the fact that we were here.

Since time eternal, women have told and retold family stories while we stir soup, wipe little noses, and comfort oldsters. We've accomplished great things, led countries, discovered radium, protected the environment, founded colleges, and crusaded against birth defects. Think Indira Gandhi, Marie Curie, Rachel Carson, Mary McLeod Bethune, and Virginia Apgar, M.D.

Closer at hand, we soothe teething babies and clean mineral deposits off faucets, make paste from flour and water in the morning and gravy thickener from water and flour in the afternoon. We know facts and events unknown by scholars and historians, possessing a tantalizing mix of information to offer others; family stories and heartbreaking secrets, like the reason cousin Maria doesn't talk to cousin Edith; the medical history of miscarriage in our family; and the reasons I was beaten as a child by my daddy.

Whether we're thirty or 100, passing on the story of our lives—the wisdom we've discovered—is important. Remember Muriel Rukeyser's question, "What would happen if one woman told the truth about her life?" I visualize the earth reacting gently to one woman's story, unfolding her reality. Then the world reverberates to the buzzing of hundreds—why not millions of women?—telling the truth of their lives. The globe moves to the magnificent hubbub of happiness, sadness, love, laughter, grieving and anger as women's words sing out, each story separate yet connected. I imagine their words on paper, the sphere trembling in anticipation as pages go flying faster and faster, spinning and turning, cream into butter, straw into gold, life into stories, until Mother Earth splits open from the pure joy of it all.

Take up your pencil and paper. Turn on your computer. Crack open your world. When the writing is finished, say, "Yes, I was here." Your stories can last as long as the paper that holds them and as long as the people who read them. Long live this endless paper trail of women's wisdom!

THE END OF SOMETHING

Sara Etgen-Baker
Dallas Branch
_sab_1529@yahoo.com_

In a village called Aerendyl there once lived an inexperienced but talented elfin scribe named Lessien Nénharma.

Now it happened one day that Lessien came upon an email message from an editor at one of the major scribal presses. With bated breath, Lessien opened the email.

> _Dearest Scribe:_
>
> _I've received your synopsis and the first two chapters of your novel. Although your scribing and story line show great promise, your characters are flat and lack humanity. Your subplots are intriguing but seem disconnected from the major plot. The narrative arc is weak, and your story has no clear ending. So, I can't accept your manuscript at this time._
>
> _Sincerely,_
>
> _Amroth Súron,_
> _Senior Editor, Drannor Press_

Lessien threw down her scribal quill and Skyped her instructor, Lady Telemmaitë.

"Lady Telemmaitë, whatever am I to do?" Lessien fought back tears. "Tell me. Is this the end of my scribal career?"

"No, my fellow scribe. Rejection doesn't mark the end of your career. Rather, rejection heralds a new beginning."

36

"You speak in riddles, Lady Telemmaitë. I don't understand!"

"'Tis quite simple, my accomplished apprentice. Toss out your old manuscript." Lady Telemmaitë leaned forward. "This time begin with the ending in mind."

"So, I focus on how the plot ends, right?"

"No, scribe, no! Focus on your characters; for your characters, their motives, and their development drive their actions and set the plot in motion—not the other way around. Begin with where they will end up."

"I understand, Lady Telemmaitë, but I feel so overwhelmed and am afraid to begin again."

"Begin one chapter at a time. Its end will determine the next one's beginning." Lady Telemmaitë smiled. "Take heart. Chapters begin and end, but fear thee not thine own endings, for they are but beginnings in disguise. Now grab thy quill and begin your next chapter!"

PART THREE:

Creative Process

WHAT IS CREATIVITY?

Dr. Patricia Daly-Lipe
DC Branch
literarylady.com

What is creativity? To find out, we can pursue two avenues. On the one hand, we can follow a systematic, methodical mode of rational thought. On the other hand, the search can be approached irrationally or non-logically, a non-linear mode of thought.

On the rational side, we begin with words. To form a description of creativity, we need a vocabulary. Or do we? Here, the right brain (the non-rational side) kicks in and challenges the left's (or rational side's) attempt at analysis. Is part of the essence of creativity beyond definition? If this is the case, can we think (and thus experience creativity) without words?

Are language and the naming of things equivalent to thinking? According to Webster, to think means "to have the mind occupied on some subject; to judge; to intend; to imagine, to consider" and "to believe." Can we imagine without imaging something? Can we believe without believing something? Prior to naming things, is man thinking?

Thinking involves knowing, and what follows is the possibility that knowing does not need an image. Perhaps to know requires that we recognize how much we do not know. To paraphrase St. Thomas: "The more that I know, the more I know how little I know." Etymology or the study of the derivation of words can assist and enhance our search for the origin of thought. The word "recognize," for example, comes from "re" (again) and *cognosere* (Latin, meaning 'to know'). Thus, if we recognize something, it is because we knew it before. But when did we begin to know? And, therefore, when did we begin to think, since thinking and knowing are mutually supporting? Again, we look at words. How do we "know," understand, and "recognize" (know again) the following words: *love*, *hate*, *envy*? These are words, but they aren't objects; they cannot be visualized. They come from within. These are called *emotions*. Our primitive ancestors probably anthropomorphized word pictures to express feelings; adjectives came later.

Metaphor pairs two images thrown into relief but intact, each unto itself. There is a definite psychological mechanism used in the processing of a metaphor. "Metaphor is probably the most fertile power possessed by man," wrote José Ortega Gassetin in 1948. For Ortega, life was an intense dialogue between oneself and one's environment. "Things are not me and I am not things: we are mutually transcendent, but both are immanent in that absolute coexistence, which is life." (*Unas lecciones de metafisica*, 1966) "*Yo soy yo y mi circumstancia*—I am I and my circumstances." Metaphor transcends the obvious and the visual; it translates man's relation to his environment on another level—a "transcendent," unique, or creative level.

Another linguistic aspect of creativity might be observed in Descartes' definition of the essence of man: "*Je pense, donc je suis*" (I think; therefore, I am) which occurs in his *Discourse on Method* (1637). Philosophical thought expresses both the potential and the limitations of human knowledge. It demands that we attempt to think beyond reality.

But how did man jump from naming names to 'understanding' them, from depicting observed images on the walls of a cave to developing philosophical insight? The answer, I believe, occurred when we became conscious of the difference between us and other; when we understood that we were 'seeing' this or that and we were somehow *involved* with what was "out there." Could it be that our awareness of ourselves in the world as other than the objects came before words? If so, the words, even the painted images, followed thought. And if this is so, thought comes before words. Man can think without words. *I am; therefore, I think*. So, the depiction of what we observed and the development of a language to express our relationship with the observed were preceded by something beyond words.

The root of the word imagination, is image. To imagine something in the mind's eye, we must have seen it in the "outside" world. The object is on the outside; the thought of the object is on the inside. However, the two sides are not separate. Sensations follow the same logic. We can feel/hear/see/smell; there is no hearing without sound, no sense-perception without an object to provoke it. Again, it is a question of the person knowing that he knows, being aware that he is aware. First there is the thought and then there is the thing. The inevitable question follows: If there were no thought of it, would the object not be there? Is an object/sensation a thing unto itself without a person's perception of it? Does thought exist before words?

Science can contribute facts; however, the philosopher (from Latin, *philos,* meaning "loving," and *Sophos,* meaning "wise") in his wide intellectual pursuit knows no boundaries.

The word 'create' means to bring forth something new as an artistic or intellectual invention. The moment preceding the act of spontaneous creativity has been described many ways. Dancer Isadora Duncan called it a "state of complete suspense." This non-verbal excitement, dreamlike, vague, and ambiguous is also experienced in the other arts: painting, writing, music, and sculpting. Author and poet Stephen Spender expressed it succinctly and pointedly as "a dim cloud of an idea, which I feel must be condensed into a shower of words." In painting, I have often experienced what Cézanne described as "an iridescent chaos" when the painting and I compete for dominance. Paint stroke by paint stroke, the colors sit up on the canvas, and the adventure begins as I attempt to come to an agreement (or image) while the painting seems to have a mind of its own. This sounds like nonsense, but for me it sets in motion my subconscious. Mesmerized, I watch as something new manifests itself on the canvas before my bewildered eyes. The same happens in creative writing, when the words take over and I am amazed.

But it is the art of music that represents a plane of consciousness beyond form and epitomizes creativity at its most abstract and pure state. In its acoustical and physical manifestation, music is imbued with mathematics. Pythagoras (c. 582 B.C. – 497 B.C.) was considered an early "scientist" and was thought to be the originator of the theory of harmonics. Fascinated with numbers and their manifestations as chords, Pythagoras is supposed to have "cured" his ailing disciples by playing music. In ancient times, music was inseparable from science mainly because of its source, mathematics. Recent studies have shown that the music of Mozart strengthens the neural connections that underline mathematical thought. So, the ancients were on to something after all. The etymology of "mathematics" is from the Greek *mathema*, meaning what is learned. Perhaps this should convince us of music as a source of creativity outside of the visible but well within the norm of analysis?

Digging into the consciousness, letting loose associations and the confines of sequential constraints and expressing an *ah-ha* moment or creative vision is not confined to the artist. Were it not for the free ranging of his imagination, Einstein could never have formulated his laws of relativity. It was in a dream, he said, that he "discovered" the basis of his insight into relativity. "Inspiration," he wrote, "is more important than knowledge." The free-roaming mind allows the scientist to "discover" things he surely would miss if he were locked into pure rationality.

To summarize, "creativity" may be viewed in this new age of fiber optics and cyberspace as an oddity, half-feared and half-distrusted but surreptitiously peeking its head out, demanding attention. The sixth sense needs to be heeded. Perhaps that is the most important function, the goal of the artist, to "transport the mind in experience past the guardians—desire and fear—to the...rapture of seeing in a single hair 'a thousand golden lions'" (Joseph Campbell). As Alfred North Whitehead concluded,

"Nature is a structure of evolving processes. The reality is the process." And equally, understanding creativity is itself a "process." Answers are not required!

A CREATIVE JOURNEY

Carol S. Mann
Palm Springs Branch
carolsmann.com

I recently made a creative journey culminating with the publication of the book *All Ways a Woman*, a collection of art and poetry celebrating women, done in collaboration with artist Lynn Centeno. As Lynn and I worked on the project, we recognized the uniqueness of every woman's life. However, we also realized a universality of experience. Women inspire and encourage each other with their strength, their resolve, and grit; with their vulnerability and ability to give; with their talents. We wanted to capture this story, these feelings.

The book, published by AquaZebra Press in hardcover, became available on Amazon in January 2017. Within its pages, we walked a woman's path, gave voice to her life song, and honored her journey. We celebrated being in all ways a woman, always.

The collaboration began in 2011, but we didn't know it. Lynn and I participated in an ekphrasis (*EHK-fra-sis*) program for writers and artists, sponsored by the Palm Springs Branch NLAPW.

Branch artists submitted their art online, and branch writers selected a work of art about which to write. I chose Lynn's watercolor, "I Care Not." For the final program, each artist's work was displayed, and the writer read her accompanying piece. By the end of the event, a calm could be felt in the room. The women in attendance, whether they knew each other or not, seemed to feel what can only be described as a palpable closeness, a bonding of spirit, and a sense of well-being. The Palm Springs Branch repeated the event in 2013, and I again chose one of Lynn's watercolors, "Girls' Night Out," to write about. Both watercolors and poems are in the book.

Three years passed. In the summer of 2016, Lynn casually suggested we do more. We each went through our body of work, searching for everything "woman." Themes came to life about thoughts, loves, and lives. Some poems had been previously published in literary journals; some watercolors had been in juried shows. We also created new work. We had a story—a woman's story.

As with any endeavor, we discovered a few tricks along the way that apply when involved in a collaborative effort:

1. Come prepared.
2. Meet commitments.
3. Respect each other's work and ideas.
4. Don't compete.
5. Respect each other's process. People have different ways of arriving at a mutually-desired result.
6. Negotiate when visions differ.
7. Compliment.
8. Listen.
9. Be flexible and stay focused. Discoveries may be made. Plans can change.
10. Recognize that during the creative process, stress and tensions may develop. (Review numbers three and five.)

Our creative journey taught us about collaborating and creating an enduring work of art. It inspired us. We hope women will become inspired by their own journey.

IT'S THE STORY THAT COUNTS

Sarah Byrn Rickman
Pikes Peak Branch
sarahbyrnrickman.com

With seven books aimed at an adult audience, all focused on women in aviation, I should stick with what I know. Right?

"Young girls need to be reading your WASP stories," two author friends told me over beers at a writers' conference last fall. "Write for them."

"But I don't know how." Deep down, I knew they were right.

The research for book number eight was done. B.J. Erickson's story would be my fourth biography and eighth book about the women pilots of World War II.

I got to know B.J. well over her final fifteen years. I visited her frequently, did her oral history, shared a speaking podium with her, and got to know her family. She "flew west" on July 7, 2013. She was 93, a great lady, and I miss her.

If ever there was a story for my fourteen-year-old granddaughter and her contemporaries, B.J.'s was it. A consummate leader at 22, she was a no-nonsense gal with keen insight into what made people tick, as evidenced by the accolades heaped on her by the women in her squadron who flew under her leadership in WWII.

I approached a friend who knows my "adult" work but who publishes for middle-grade readers. I asked if she would be interested in publishing a WASP biography for Y/A and, if so, would she work with me to get it right? She agreed.

Six weeks later, I had the first draft. Something built a fire under me!

My editor sent back her suggestions. I took them to heart and began draft two. My multi-clause sentences painstakingly became two or three stand-alone sentences. I searched for easier-to-understand synonyms—tough for aviation terms that the average adult reader won't know, let alone a thirteen-year-old. When in doubt, explain.

Oh, yes—I also had a 25,000-word limit. I'm used to 80,000. Focus. I got my 30,000 down to 25,000.

My journalist's training has taught me to write short paragraphs. That helped. But because we're dealing with a lot of B.J.'s quotes, I've had to alternate them with paraphrasing because of the way the book would be formatted. I never had to worry about that before!

I removed my proverbial darlings and that pesky dead wood—several times.

There were far too many dates and airplane numbers. Too much for young readers! Historian, ditch your dates. They're boring!

I submitted draft three. The story was told. I'd tightened the lens. Enough?

No. Don't start planning the cover yet. Revisions, not major but nevertheless needed, were required.

I thought I could do it in six months, start to finish—November to April. It was not ready in April, nor in May.

On July 11, I handed the finished manuscript—25,745 words—to my editor, Doris Baker of the small Colorado book publisher Filter Press.

The cover is now a go, and it is gorgeous. It is B.J. in the cockpit of a P-51 World War II fighter aircraft.

In all, 63 photos grace this book aimed at eleven to fourteen-year-old girls and, hopefully, boys. Boys do like aviation.

B.J. was 19 when she learned to fly, right before World War II began. She qualified as a flight instructor at age 20 and, after Pearl Harbor, joined the Women's Auxiliary Ferrying Squadron (WAFS) to fly small trainer aircraft from the factory to the Army training fields.

These women become known as WASP (Women Airforce Service Pilots). At 22, B.J. was named the leader of the women's ferrying squadron in Long Beach, California. She led some 70 other women, many older than she, for the two years the WASP were on active duty.

Her squadron was the one tasked with the delivery of the largest number of P-51 fighter aircraft delivered by the women pilots. The P-51 was THE aircraft—the "Game Changer"—that ultimately sealed our victory over the German Reich in 1945. The P-51 was the aircraft that protected the big bombers from enemy fighters all the way from England to Berlin, then back to England and safety.

It's the story that counts—and yes, how you tell it. Writing, whether for adults or for children, is all about whether you tell the story in a way that engages your reader, puts her right there in the cockpit with the heroine, and brings both the pilot and the story home.

Photo of B.J. Erickson, page 47, supplied by Sarah Byrn Rickman.

SWIMMING UPSTREAM

Bonnie Jo Smith
Santa Clara County Branch
bonniejofiberarts.com

In 1999, I suffered a work-related injury. Being told that I might never be active on my feet or work the job I so enjoyed again, and that I would have to use a wheelchair, was a shock I didn't handle well.

Having to sit 100% of the time in 2001, I decided to take a quilting class. I thought creating a few heirlooms for my family would be a nice gesture. Well, quilt I did—and to the frustration of my teacher, I could not stay within the pattern. My thought was, why do I want to create something that looked like everyone else's?

Having moved to a new home with a lot of empty walls, I informed my husband that we'd purchase no new art; I would create art for our walls. Create, I did. My work has now traveled the globe, been juried into the prestigious Quilt National, and is held in private collections—and I feel like I'm just warming up.

For many years, I wondered how to translate that unrelenting horrific situation of my work injury into my artwork, but always avoided the subject in my art.

After I sat and let my body heal, the doctors said, "You can start exercising."

"How about swimming?" I asked.

Thereafter, I swam every day.

One day, my youngest daughter Shara purchased me a pair of swim fins. Well, I had my doubts. Within about eight months, however, I witnessed a remarkable change in my feet. I then realized that those fins were probably the best physical therapy I could have had. The fins forced my feet to rebuild the muscle. I knew I was on my way.

While enjoying my swims, I would imagine what an artwork of myself swimming would look like. Could I create it? Would viewers accept my minimalist creative style or reject my work?

I rarely shy away too long from taking on a task, so I created *Swimming Upstream:*

I looked at the finished work for a long time. It came to me that the artwork was not just about myself; it's about everyone trying to navigate through life. For some, it's hard to pick up the pieces and keep swimming upstream. For others, it's just about trying to survive life.

Ideas keep coming to me for new works. Some show how we have days when we feel strong, and then other days when we need to pull back, maybe feeling just a little too much hubris. This series has been fun to create and visualize how I feel about myself moving onward and upward. People have gravitated to this work, as swimming is an iconic image that most of us can do or try.

I tell those who want to swim but say they can't to just float or hold onto the side of the pool. One day, you will get the courage to let go and feel your body enjoy the stability that the water—or the world—can offer, depending on how you see it. Even if you never try swimming, you can always imagine yourself swimming upstream through life. Just imagine!

Image of "Swimming Upstream," page 51, supplied by Bonnie Jo Smith.

MY CREATIVE WORKSPACE

Marsha J. Perlman
Southwest Florida Branch
www.marshajperlman.com

My inspiration for writing comes from the vast natural environment that surrounds me. My work space is the outdoors, and I am an "outdoors person."

Living part of the year in the foothills of the Rocky Mountains assures me no shortage of poetry subjects. My backpack carries a notebook, pencils, a ruler, a small shovel, a covered plastic container, a canteen, a snack, a rain jacket, and a camera.

I choose a topic and spend blocks of time observing and taking notes as I move around the area by bike and foot. Or I choose a destination that is more flexible and allows for returning often to view changes that occur.

When I take many notes in the field, there is occasionally the problem of not recalling the sensory data. Therefore, I immediately describe the words that I can't retrace later, such as bird songs. Before I leave my subject, I scan my notes to be certain I have all the information I need. Sometimes, I take a few photos.

Once at home I sit at my desk and, in pencil, write the first draft of my new poem. I read it aloud several times for obvious changes in grammar, spelling, punctuation, or repetitive words. Printing is next, and then I set the work aside for a week.

When I am ready to revise, I ask another person to read the poem aloud. Then I reread and rethink the text several times again, each time with a fresh eye for accepting, eliminating, or adding another new word choice, better sentence structure, or organization.

I often return to the location of the poem, if it is available, and ask myself if I need to rework any lines. If so, I repeat the process. I want to be certain all my ideas are clear to the reader.

WE ARE WHAT WE CREATE: A MEMOIR OF A LATTER-DAY SAINT

Laura Walth
Des Moines Branch
laura.walth@gmail.com

A phrase my brother Phil often liked to repeat during our Sunday morning phone conversations was "Out of the bad comes the good." Phil so desperately wanted me to finish my memoir, to know what life was like for the eight years before he was born. He also felt there was a story that needed to be shared.

He had no idea about the struggles I put myself through to get to where I am today. He wanted to know it all. He instinctively knew he didn't have much longer to live but denied death to hear my story and know how it was going to end.

Phil and I were never very close growing up. He annoyed me to the point that I didn't like being around him.

When he was in 2nd grade and our parents were out of town, I got so mad at him I kicked a hole through his bedroom door and knocked his pet, Myrtle the turtle, to the floor. I felt sorrier for my grandmother, who was taking care of us; she didn't know what to do. I didn't know how to explain what had just happened. It scared both my brother and me.

After that, we just left each other alone. I found out much later in life that he was afraid of me yet always admired me as his big sister.

In 1995, I received a call from my sister Bertie in South Dakota. Phil was in the VA hospital and not expected to live. He had been diagnosed with AIDS and had pneumonia. We all went to say our goodbyes.

We were prepared for his death, but Phil wasn't ready to give up on life. He later told us it was the love he felt from us that gave him the desire to live.

We had to find a place for him to live because we weren't prepared to have him live with us in his condition. We found him a group home to stay in, but he decided to move into an apartment with someone he'd met at that place for the terminally ill. His new friend wanted to experience life rather than wait to die. They moved to Arizona, where his friend died a year later.

Phil eventually moved to Florida, where he lived with AIDS for many years. He survived cancer, a staph infection that could have killed a healthy person, and pneumonia several times throughout his life. It was a stroke that left him unable to walk or talk and took away his quality of life, yet he chose to hang on. Ten days before he passed away, my sisters and I let him know it was okay to let go. We expressed our love for him over the phone. I made a promise to finish my memoir and then wondered what good that would do if he wasn't here to see the finished product.

Having faith that there is life after death gives me the belief that his spirit lives on and my story needs to be shared. It feels like his spirit is present as these words come to me in the process of sharing my life experience. Making that promise to him made me believe that he'd be the muse I needed to create a life story for a book.

That's how I arrived at the title for my memoir.

I have wanted to be a Saint since childhood, but I was not born into the Mormon faith. My husband and I moved from North Dakota to New York in 1974. In 1982 a Jewish friend of ours and his Christian girlfriend discovered something that they said changed their lives. We were curious to know more, and we found what we were looking for. They didn't join the LDS Religion, but we did. Mom joined several years later.

Phil was very concerned for us. He thought for sure we'd joined a cult and had convinced Mom to join as well. Then he saw a positive change in Mom. She no longer needed a drink to calm her once-troubled soul. She found peace and joy in life without the alcohol. Later, he told me it was the best thing that ever happened to her.

The conflict taking place in California between the Mormons and the gay community was what brought my brother and I together. It was called Proposition Eight and regarded same-sex marriage. A commercial was made that depicted Mormon missionaries in a very bad light. It bothered me so much, I called my brother to ask what he thought about what was said about Mormons in this commercial. He said he was upset that the gay community was wasting good money that could have been spent on far worthier causes than bashing Mormons for their beliefs.

That phone call changed our relationship for good. We found a common ground that let us open up about past experiences that kept us apart for so many years. We discovered that it was fear that kept us from communicating: He was afraid of me, and I was afraid of him.

We became friends. He called me on Sundays before I went to church. When I was teaching Sunday school, I would share my lesson with him, and when I was asked to give a talk at church, I would share that with him. He would give me feedback.

While looking for photos of my brother, I found the two that follow. On the left is my father, and on the right is my brother:

I never realized how much Phil looked like our father until I saw these pictures. Like me, Phil also felt he could never please Dad no matter what he did, including joining the 82nd Airborne.

One time, Phil told me I'd brought tears of joy to him because he finally understood that my religion is about service and compassion. He felt my love for him, and he understood that it was more about love than being judgmental of others.

So, he visited an LDS church service in Florida to learn more. Phil then shared how much he'd enjoyed learning more about the religion through the Sister Missionaries he invited to his home. He wasn't ready to make a commitment to membership, but at least he was willing to find out more. Whenever anyone in the gay community would start Mormon-bashing, he defended the faith. He was proud to tell them that his sister was a Mormon.

At first, I thought it a bit presumptuous to think of myself as a Saint. My life experience has helped me see how being an overachiever was a way to compensate for feelings of inadequacy. Writing my memoir has helped me change my mind.

I can replace negative thoughts with positive ones about the image I want to create. It's not easy, living the life of a Saint, but it's a fun challenge.

To fulfill this calling means being a person who is good, kind, and patient. I can be recognized as a Saint because of the way I live the rest of my life. If *we are what we create,* then I will truly strive to be a Latter-Day Saint. That doesn't mean I'm perfect; it's just something to aspire to before the end of my life on Earth. It's a work in progress.

We Are What We Create: A Memoir of a Latter-Day Saint won't just be about the Mormon religion; it will be a story about the life experience that led me to where I am today.

Phil always encouraged me to be a leader. He liked how I listened to both sides of a story and didn't judge others for their beliefs. My brother would have been thrilled to hear about my involvement with the National League of American Pen Women.

Family photographs on page 58 supplied by Laura Walth.

PART FOUR:

Creative Wisdom

THE CALL

Mary Joan Meagher
Minnesota Branch
maryjoanmeagher@gmail.com

What did you do on your last birthday? If you became 40 or 50 years old, you probably had a stressful day. A comedic cousin, friend, or even a spouse might have thought that it would be fun to tease you about your age.

Perhaps someone threw you a surprise party at work. Everyone showed up wearing black clothes. They gave you a cake with black and white frosting that featured a grave with your name printed on a headstone emblazoned with the initials "R.I.P." Everybody laughed and thought it was hilariously funny... until it happened to them.

Birthdays are hard enough without someone else taking them over and telling you how to feel. We all mark the passage of time in different ways, but it is always a time of account-keeping. We think about our faces and bodies, and we measure them against what we remember we looked like at sixteen or twenty.

This exercise is usually detrimental. Your spirits sink as you consider wrinkles, gray hairs, and double chins, or notice the effect that too many fast food stops have had on your waistline.

One saving measure to take at zero birthdays (when you enter a new decade) is to do another kind of accounting. Take a measure of how far you have moved in getting closer to your goals.

Dean Koontz, a best-selling novelist, says he writes and edits ten pages each day. What are your goals? Have you kept your promise to yourself to write or create something new each day? Have you finished a chapter of your novel?

You need to get in touch with your inner self. You need to listen to your inner voice. For this exercise, set up a quiet space of time on your birthday. Get up earlier than normal. Find a quiet peaceful place either inside or outside, in the house or in the park, in the library or in the woods. This is your day. Find your place and time.

When you learn how to listen to your inner voice, you will know what you are called to do at this time in your life. Each stage of your life has a different calling. If you are too tuned-in to the voices of others constantly deciding your fate every 24 hours, when can you ever know what is right for you? Go back to your youthful dreams. What were you called to do then? What were you looking for? What were you going to be?

Your birthday can be a wonderful experience if you use it to launch a new enterprise, to take the first step to improving your relationships with others, to listen to the voice within calling you to be all you can be. Cyril Connolly, critic and editor, said: "Better to write for yourself and have no public than to write for the public and have no self."

SELF CULTURE: BEING WITHOUT SPEAKING

Elizabeth Diane Garcia Martin
Pikes Peak Branch
12phases.com

If there is one thing constant in human nature, it is that each of us reduces the chaos outside of us by creating a highly personal and private environment of one human being: yourself.

There is no straight path in the swirl held in our private premises. We humans are a rolling conundrum of apparent contradictions, living life at four levels—intellectually, emotionally, physically and spiritually—automatically and intuitively. This *self-culture* ensures the survival of personal identity, what distinguishes you from all other persons.

Individuality is the source of original work. Whether it is in the arts or in the subtler expressions of love and devotion, originality is the gift each woman brings into her life and out to the lives of others. If creativity is to be understood, the internal experience of a person must be understood.

CREATING FLOW

A natural inner navigation system works for us to maintain ownership of our identities. In hindsight, we see this more clearly. To get a feel for the path your life unconsciously indicates, take time to review your life. Paint your life history with broad strokes by taking note of how you felt at the end of 12-year phases: at age 12; age 24; age 36, and so on. Identify major decisions you made about life, based on your experiences up to that point. Linked together, these turning points are clues to your identity.

The flow of life comes when the heart, mind, soul, and body are united in purpose. The heart and spirit are anchored *outside* of time, and that attachment to timeless intangible values keeps us on course with meaning. It is the reaching from the heart that goes beyond the physical world and draws us toward inspiration that fuels life.

This is why creativity has the power to affect others at an unconscious level—heart to heart. As you pick up on the unconscious movement of your life, you will mature into the purpose you were born with and become comfortable with expressing it.

Through self-evaluation and realizing the value system anchored in your living history, you align your mind with natural, instinctive creativity.

NATURAL, INSTINCTIVE CREATIVITY

Our natural tendency is to lean forward, toward the future. It's that leaning forward that is the basis of love. What stirs the heart toward love is unconscious, self-renewing, positive and unquenchable. You are willing to extend yourself in the direction your heart is stirred. Extending yourself – exposing your true self – increases love. Beauty in art, music and artful writing cultivates love. Childlike innocence, kindness, and friendship are things that encourage us to "lean forward," to take chances in life.

Leaning forward is the subtle guiding influence in our hearts, and it speaks to the unconscious mind in whispers. Unrealized intentions are held in the subconscious, waiting for an opportunity or the right time to be carried out. Involuntary response is love that acts without checking in with your conscious mind, and love will always win, no matter how long it takes.

Inspiration breathes life into your heart, first, and then invigorates your whole being. Heart motivation makes work light, and you become renewed as you work. This is the life of a creative person.

Workers in the arts find that life's "downs" enhance its "ups" in a way that refines our perception of good, or identifies the un-good in contrast, or puts joy and loss together in a place where they complement each other.

To be yourself requires enormous strength. In the heart is the strength we need for a lifetime: strength to endure, to overcome, to grow, to create, and to be happy. All that you are fits perfectly in your life and makes it unique. Allow it. Lean into the good and create!

A JOURNEY INTO THE HEART OF CREATIVITY

Dr. Patricia Daly-Lipe
DC Branch
literarylady.com

Maybe I am a late bloomer, but finally I have arrived at an important juncture in my life. What I used to consider a pastime, I now consider a passion. Two creative arts, painting and writing, have become the focus of my life.

I crept slowly into taking my art seriously. As a child, I watched my father paint. I learned to use watercolors when a woman down the street from my home in California opened her house to the neighborhood children and taught painting. Often, we would take our tablets down to the rocks and attempt to paint images of the incoming surf.

Later I attended the local Art Center's painting classes for children in a little white wooden building with trellises laced with flowering Wisteria vines in front. My work won at some shows, but for me, art was just a pleasant thing to do.

I took art classes in school and later in college, but still it was not enough of a passion to warrant full-time study. As a young adult, I studied figure drawing. My likenesses were quite good, but the paintings lacked depth. They were more like caricatures or illustrations. I came to find between years of learning to draw figures with proper proportions and dimensions, tones and contrasts, and learning to paint with style, my own style, there exists a leap of faith. It takes knowing how to draw things and people as they really are to be able to draw or paint them as they appear to you the artist—and knowing who you are is the center piece of creativity.

Vincent Van Gogh said it best. In 1879, he wrote: "I know of no better definition of the word 'art' than this: 'Art is man added to nature,' nature, reality, truth, but with a significance, a conception, with a character which the artist makes evolve, and to which he expresses, that he frees up, illuminates." I believe deep down within our very being lives the creative muse, and she is yearning to find expression. It is she who connects to the primal rhythms of the universe. Watching a sunset, looking at the snow-covered bare limbs of a tree, peering into the opened petals of a rose, all these scenes are captured by our creative muse, who stores them in our memory. Someday, she will find release. That is, if we allow it.

But creativity is not confined to art. The writer, be he or she a novelist or historian, a biographer or a reporter, also allows creativity to find expression. For the writer the words paint the picture. Consider poetry. Poetry celebrates feelings. "No tears in the writer; no tears in the reader," Robert Frost said. This is true of the poem and equally true of literature. Just as "a poem begins with a lump in the throat," so too a good book should entice the soul, draw upon the emotions and require reflection.

The artist considers the media to use; the writer chooses the words. There is an affinity between musical rhythm and literary rhythm: repetition/meter/movement/harmony. One of the most powerful mimes defining life is sound. Take the 'motion' out of 'emotion.' Music is motion. Life is motion. For some, the creative muse finds her expression in music. Words are not necessary. The visual is not necessary. Music takes us beyond the external world and draws upon our inner selves, our emotions.

So be it writing, art or music. "Within each of us is a creative core that actively creates the universe," Robert Hand said.

Man is both creature and creator. Creative energy creates. The journey never ends, and it is the journey, not its destination, and the creating, not the created, that opens our minds and hearts to more than logic, science, or technology can ever know.

PROPRIOCEPTIVE WRITING:
A COMMUNICATION LOOP

Bobbie Dumas Panek
Central New York Branch
bobbiedumaspanek.com

"From a voice in your head, to your arm and hand as you write, to your voice as you read what you've written, to your ears as you hear what your voice has to say. It's that simple."

As a writer, poet, and author I enjoy being inspired and motivated, and I enjoy hanging out with like-minds. I look for writing workshops where I know I will work on my favorite skill while I'm with creative people. A recent writing retreat that I attended is one that I'd like to share with others. It was so incredibly wonderful, it's hard to describe—but here goes.

I'd first heard about Proprioceptive Writing from my twin sister, Beckie, who lives in the Adirondacks. She's friends with Ann Mullen, who is a Proprioceptive Writing (PW) Teacher. Beckie had attended one of Ann's weekend workshops and relayed to me how it "works." I then read the book, *Writing the Mind Alive*, written by Linda Trichter Metcalf, PhD. and Toby Simon, PhD.

The sub-title for *Writing the Mind Alive*, is "The Proprioceptive Method for Finding Your Authentic Voice." Now, I know the word *proprioceptive* is odd. Who knows what it means, and how can it help you with your authentic voice?

According to the dictionary programmed onto my MacBook Air:

> **proprioceptive** |prōprēə'septiv| (adjective) *Physiology*
> - *relating to stimuli that are produced and perceived within an organism, especially those connected with the*

position and movement of the body. Compare with exteroceptive and interoceptive.

There is no similar word according to the thesaurus (I told you this would be hard to describe), but here is how I learned:

- I bought and reread the book, *Writing the Mind Alive,* "The Proprioceptive Method for Finding Your Authentic Voice"
- I signed up for a 5-day Immersive *PW* writing retreat taught by Ann Mullen and Anne Bright

Seventeen of us showed up at this Retreat Center called Wisdom House in Litchfield, Connecticut. (Workshops are on both coasts of the United States and in Holland.) The website, if you want to look for more, is http://pwriting.org.

- I met many wonderfully creative people
- I learned a skill that I'll apply for the rest of my life
- I can attest this method brings clarification and grace to my life
- The grace happened in the room where personal writes were read aloud
- The clarification occurs each time I apply the writing method, listen to each thought in my mind, write it down, question my thought when I feel the urge by asking myself, "What do I mean by...?" and then asking myself four questions at the end of each 25-minute write

Okay, now—you're perhaps even more confused by this method of writing, but I assure you it works. I'm thrilled. I feel more grounded than ever before. I listen to my voice(s); I give them space and learn from myself what I need, want, think and truly care about.

Too often, our culture is chaotic with constant chatter on-line, at home, in the car, in our heads. It is such a balm to settle down, to slow down, to think clearly and to listen to my thoughts. Trying to describe the method is like trying to describe a "gut" feeling.

The main message I'd like to share is to try this technique. Buy the book or attend at least a weekend workshop, apply this practice to your creative life, and see what happens. It works wonders. Oh, and one more thing: I'd love to hear your feedback.

PLAN B AND A PRAYER

Dorothy Atkins
Santa Clara County Branch
dorothyatkinsartist.com

While working my career job, I always had a Plan B and a prayer. Traveling 90 minutes every day by train, I'd write down a plan of what I'd rather do in life. I made a chalkboard at home with notes, inspirational quotes, and ideas of what my life would look like doing the things I loved. As a project manager, I wrote a plan for myself on a large, lined tablet. I must have used a ton of them over the years. I still look at my first outline of what I wanted to accomplish and marvel at how many things in my plan I did.

I put a big round circle in the middle of the page and smaller circles all around it with arrows pointing to the big circle. The big circle was my end goal; the smaller circles all around it was what I needed to do. I set out to do things that I could immediately work on (e.g. Who was my target audience, what did I have that no one was offering, etc.). Even though I didn't know exactly when my dreams would happen, I knew that I had to be ready for when they did. I wanted to make greeting cards and be a motivational speaker, encouraging women to follow their dreams. By writing down my dreams and wish list, along with my research and readiness, I put it out in the universe and asked for guidance.

First, I had to motivate myself:

I had conversations with my inner self, using words I had read somewhere: "Choose safe, gentle souls who are willing not to criticize you but to support you in your journey." Let them be thrilled with you; listen and hear what they're saying. Do not dismiss their compliments or encouragement.

- Ask yourself what makes you feel alive.

- Avoid balloon poppers (people who do not wish you well).

- Trust in your instincts!

- Learn, learn, learn.

- Know your audience!

- Ask why others would want you or your product.

- Be scared, but don't let fear keep you from trying. Give fear a name and take away its power.

- Talk lovingly to yourself.

What I continue to practice is confidence in what I'm doing. I'm always tapping into my creative side. I realize that I love what I do, and this keeps me motivated. It's important to challenge myself to learn new things. Exposure is a key element to my success as a speaker and artist, and although I work from home, I go to work every day and work with passion!

PART FIVE:

Creative Business

MAKE SURE YOU'RE "LEGIT"

Rodika Tollefson
Member-at-Large
Rodikat.com

If you're one of those creatives who enjoys the business side of things, congratulations! You are part of a very small group of people who love accounting and marketing as much as they love creating their art.

For the rest of us, the business aspects of paid creative work are tedious—which means we put them off for as long as we can.

You may be able to procrastinate when it comes to posting your receipts or updating your website. But there are a few things you should not postpone, and that is to make sure that you are conducting business according to the applicable local, state, and federal laws.

As soon as you decide to sell your work, you're a self-employed owner of a business. Even if you're a *solopreneur*—without an incorporated business—and you don't have a business name, you're still liable for licenses, permits, and taxes.

Here are a few things you need to know:

Business licenses: Requirements vary from state to state and, in some cases, you don't need one until you meet a certain revenue threshold. Even if you don't reach that number, a business license is a good idea for those planning to do public commissions, sell to the public, and so on.

In addition to the state, some local jurisdictions such as cities require business licenses. Some must be renewed every year.

Income taxes: The IRS may consider your business a hobby for the first few years if you don't have net income, but your state may not.

In Washington state, where I live, the business and occupation tax is based on gross income, which means businesses must pay taxes whether they actually net anything. There are very few deductions, and none of them apply to the typical writer or artist. Instead, the state has credits, on a sliding scale, for businesses that earn up to a certain amount.

Sales and personal property taxes: If you're selling tangible items like art, you will likely be liable for sales taxes. That means you must collect them from your customers, keep track, then remit them to your tax entity (typically the state).

In some states, sales tax is based not on where the sale originates, but on the shipping destination. Talk about an accounting nightmare if you're selling and shipping to customers in other locations!

Some jurisdictions also tax businesses on their inventory and personal property like equipment. My county does this, though luckily the total of my equipment value is low enough to meet the exempt criteria.

Home business permits: Some local jurisdictions require a special permit for conducting business out of your home, especially if customers will be stopping by or the business will generate noise (a chainsaw-carving artist, perhaps?). Check with your city or county.

There may be other odds and ends for you to consider based on your own location. Penalties and back taxes are no fun, so make sure you do your research.

No one dreams of having to study tax code and business regulations in order to sell creative works—but if that's what it takes to have the freedom and privilege of pursuing one's passion, I'd trade a little accounting headache for punching a time clock in an office tour any day.

BUSINESS OR UNCONDITIONAL LOVE

Ronni Miller
Sarasota Branch
writeitout.com

Business? What did I know about business? I had been a stay-at-home mother, raising three children after graduation from Boston University with a liberal arts degree, and before that I was a sheltered daughter from a middle class Jewish family whose father was a lawyer and mother was an in-the-closet artist and writer.

Determination to achieve *whatever it was you wanted* had been the operative narrative around the dining room table in my home of origin. All I ever wanted was to write, publish, marry and raise a family. Writing had been my mainstay, my plumb line since I was six years old.

Motherhood absorbed my energies, while creativity found a home in children's plays I wrote for my children's school and short stories that were stuffed in file folders. The feminist movement lit my fire, and I began to write articles and essays about the need for women to aspire to their creative potentials. A divorce propelled me into teaching English and theater in a private school, where I continued to hone my experiences by writing curriculum for my sixth and seven grade English courses. Trained in acting, I taught drama. That led to my initiation of a yearly consortium drama festival for six private schools in northern New Jersey, which gave students an opportunity to showcase their talents.

I left teaching and landed jobs editing local newspapers and magazines, continued freelance writing and publishing in local and regional publications, and acquired rejections from national magazines that shook my confidence. All the while, I continued to raise my now high school-aged kids.

I worked as a temporary secretary while my children attended college, which helped supplement a freelance income so that I could finish my first novel. An epiphany happened after years of struggles to survive that led to my Write It Out® service product, now entering its twenty-fifth year. As founder and director, I facilitate workshops in the U.S., Bermuda, and Italy, guiding individuals to express feelings, memories, and experiences through writing. In my private practice as Book Midwife, I coach individuals to birth their books.

I'm thankful every day for that epiphany. My students and clients have been my inspiration and motivate me to continue offering services. The Program has segued into the healthcare field; it's used by people affected by cancer as well as those who have suffered loss and life-altering conditions, who want to document their stories in prose, poetry, and theater pieces. Seven published books remind me that joy of creating is a balm to my spirit.

Five suggestions to others:

- **Dedicate** yourself and believe in your product or service.
- **Trust** yourself to pursue a dream.
- **Rely** on desire as your support system.
- **Listen** and observe your efforts as an educational experience.
- **Incorporate** your life experiences into a new profession.

I've translated the word *business,* still foreign to me, to mean *service*. That has made all the difference. You can call it *business*, *service*, *profession* or simply *unconditional love*. I call it being an entrepreneur.

TO FREELANCE OR NOT TO FREELANCE? 'TIS NOT AN EASY ANSWER...

Rodika Tollefson
Member-at-Large
Rodikat.com

Ahh, the freelance life. Have you been dreaming of being your own boss, working in your pajamas, and playing hooky whenever the muse abandons you?

There's certain romanticism about "working for yourself." Turning every day into casual Friday (PJs or otherwise), picking and choosing your projects, and making your own schedule sounds appealing, indeed—and that sweet 30-second commute to the office can't be beat.

But the freelance life has just as many drawbacks as advantages. If you're thinking about making the leap, make sure you know what you're getting into.

When I started the freelance life more than 15 years ago, I wanted flexibility while the kids were young. Little did I know about the "feast or famine" that's inherent with self-employment, or the other costs of "flexibility."

I've dabbled a few times since then with the idea of getting a "real" (i.e. full-time) job but despite the potential perks—paid vacation and sick leave, medical insurance, stable paycheck, and consistent hours—I hope I never have go back to "punching the clock." Once you've been self-employed for a while, it's tough to go back!

If freelancing full-time is on your mind, let's talk about some pros and cons:

Being your own boss: Don't like having a boss? Try having a dozen! Although customers can't tell you how, when, and what to do, you are accountable to every single one of them through your deliverables. They don't always listen to your expertise either—but, as the cliché goes, the customer's always right.

To add to the pressure, clients often have competing priorities and deadlines. It's up to you to meet them all.

On the other hand, being your own boss means you're in charge of your own opportunities. If you have the self-drive and motivation to succeed, this is a wonderful thing.

Setting your own schedule: So long, vacation requests at the mercy of the HR manager! You can take time off whenever you please.

That is, until several requests pour in at the same time—which, says Murphy's Law, happens more often than you may like, especially when you're in the middle of packing for that extended weekend.

The beauty of working your own schedule is that nobody cares if you work in the wee hours of morning or late at night (well, maybe your family does). You can work from the beach and even from the other side of the country or world (I did that several times, and no one was the wiser).

Choosing your projects: You can turn down a potential client or project any time you want. But in reality, you're not likely to do that regularly unless you're so renowned in your field that you can command top dollar or earn a good living with just a few gigs here and there.

Remember that "feast or famine" nobody warned me about? After 15 years of doing this, it's still not uncommon.

Take last month, for example. I was enjoying the slower pace the first week, even thinking I'd finally have time to do some creative writing, which doesn't pay the bills like my commercial work does. And then, the floodgates opened, and I spent the next three weeks camped in my home office, working 60 or more hours a week.

I could have turned down some of the projects, but they were all wonderful, new opportunities that could become long-term, well-paying projects. So, I marched on. Besides, nobody's paying for my time off—so making "extra" is a good way to finance that dream vacation.

Running your business: Whether you're a freelance writer like me or an artist, musician, or any other type of creative, working for yourself means you're running a *bona fide* business.

On the positive side, that means you can deduct business expenses like furniture for your home office and mileage. On the other hand, you have to pay oodles of taxes, as well as cover all your expenses, from equipment and professional development to marketing.

Without a regular paycheck, you must plan your cash flow carefully. Even if you think you're well prepared for the ebb and flow, all it takes to feel unstable is a longtime client pulling the plug.

I can't tell you how many times I got a phone call or email informing me that a project I've done for years was moved "in-house" or defunded, or an ongoing monthly project was canceled without any notice—sometimes more than one project in the same month.

Freelancing doesn't just take a certain kind of free spirit and self-motivation. To succeed, you need to be resilient, dogged, and thick-skinned. If you need stability, this is not the path for you.

But if you can handle some rough seas, *bon voyage*! You'll be the captain of your own ship (as well as the first mate and deckhand), and where your great new adventure takes you is completely up to you.

EIGHT STEPS TO BETTER PROFITABILITY

Katie Turner
Central New York Branch
ktartstudio.com

Turning your creative business into a profit-making enterprise can be a great challenge. The balance between time spent creating and time spent developing your business is definitely something you'll be challenged with, but once you get this balance under control, you'll start to see results.

Here are eight tips that will help put your creative business in the black:

STEP 1: Have a strong, consistent body of works. In other words, display your best paintings and leave the rest home. Not that perfection is the goal, but you should present a product that you're really proud of and can stand behind. Ask yourself if you're presenting a cohesive body of works. Can customers get a sense of you as an artist? When people feel like they understand you and your style, they're more likely to buy.

STEP 2: Optimize for individual buyers. This is where knowing your customer can really help. Many artists have a variety of sizes and prices, and they sell more than just originals. Some artists sell prints, giclées, magnets, bookmarks, posters, scarves, and more. Giving customers options is good for business.

STEP 3: Create daily. Post daily. If you're creating regularly, you have new work to post regularly. Using social media to promote your product gives potential customers an excuse to visit your shop. (It's probably not a good idea to post a lot of items at once, though; that overwhelms people.)

STEP 4: Add the tags. When using social media, be sure to use relevant tags and descriptions. What is the sense of having beautiful artwork that nobody can locate? When tagging or writing descriptions, think about what a customer might search for when looking for something like your product.

A cautionary note: *Don't do "keyword stuffing."* This is where people tag everything just to get a lot of short-term views on their product. Google bots recognize this and penalize you by keeping you out of search results. A potential customer could find your product and see no relationship between what you've tagged and what the actual content of your artwork is, and it leaves a bad taste. Don't give the customer a reason to avoid you.

STEP 5: Share your products. Don't be afraid to put your products out there on Facebook, Instagram, Pinterest, Tumblr, Snapchat, etc. By letting your network know you have great new products, you're keeping them interested. If you're concerned about theft, limit your images to smaller sizes and use a copyright symbol with your name embedded in the image. Tutorials are available online to help with embedding copyrights.

STEP 6: Give 'em what they want. If you're getting a lot of orders or "likes" on a specific style item, why not keep your customers happy with more similar products? On a side note, remember to put out products that are relevant to the season— for example: back-to-school, college gear, Christmas or holiday times. Work 4-8 weeks in advance in order to give customers time to pick up your product and then have time to deliver it before the holiday.

STEP 7: Have Marketing Materials. This probably goes without saying, but make sure you always have a business card on you. You never know when you will meet a new customer. Hand out postcards of your work and include your website on the back.

STEP 8: Plan your goals. It's so easy for a creative individual to get distracted. Having a written business plan and daily goals can really help. Setting goals is also a great way to control your time (artistically and otherwise) and you'll find you won't waste as much time or money aimlessly.

 Making a living off your art can be a challenging job. You'll end up spending a lot of time hustling the business side of it, but it's all worth it when you realize you're doing what you love.

HOW TO USE COPYRIGHT-FREE IMAGES AND SOUND WITHOUT GETTING IN TROUBLE

Rodika Tollefson
Member-at-Large
Rodikat.com

If you create art for a living, you probably feel strongly about protecting your copyrights. After all, even if all that sweat and tears went into the work for the pleasure of it, you have bills to pay.

I am constantly surprised how many creatives don't think twice when the tables are turned. They think it's perfectly okay to copy a photo from a news or stock site, or an image from social media, and use it for their own website, brochure, etc.; use a song purchased from iTunes for a video promoting their art, event, etc.; or re-purpose someone else's painting for their book's cover.

Paying 99 cents for a song for your personal music library doesn't mean you can legally use it as a soundtrack for that great video promo you're making, and just because it's easy to copy and paste an image from a website or someone shared a photo on Facebook doesn't mean you can take it for your own use.

This also applies to images from historic archives, including the Library of Congress, because they often have a copyright holder. In these cases, all you may need is to ask permission. Get it in writing!

What's a creative with a limited budget to do in all other cases? If you need free music or images, look either for works in the public domain, or for those that have a Creative Commons license. Many photographers, musicians and artists — even professionals — freely allow others to use their work, often only in exchange for attribution.

Some sources of free music:

- Incompetech.com (my personal favorite for indie short documentaries)
- Musopen.org (public domain music including recordings of classical music)
- Freemusicarchive.org (make sure to read the details in the license guide)
- YouTube's free music library (for YouTube videos only)
- Audionautix.com

Some sources of free images:

- flickr Creative Commons
- Wikimedia's Creative Commons or public domain (use the search bar at the top, and read carefully about each image's copyright)
- 123rf.com/browsefreeimages.php —the choices are limited, but you can also buy credits in small increments from 123rf.com and use them toward individual images (it comes down to as low as $1 per image, depending on the size/resolution you need); this is my go-to site to buy stock art for The Pen Woman
- New York Public Library's public domain collection
- stockvault.net
- Unsplash.com/collections

Read the license terms carefully because even a Creative Commons license may have restrictions and specific requirements on how to give the artist credit. Some don't allow use for commercial purposes—and even if you're not making any money from the product, your purpose may still be considered commercial. If you can't give attribution to the artists, many of them will let you use their work for a small fee instead.

One final point: Don't let by the term "royalty-free" mislead you. It doesn't mean "free to take." Chances are, you need to pay a licensing fee, which comes with certain terms, just like Creative Commons (it may restrict use to news purposes, may require author credit even if you're paying for the image, and may disallow any editing).

And, of course, don't forget the best resource of all: fellow Pen Women. You may have a composer or photographer in your own branch who would be happy to share her work with you.

(*Disclaimer: I'm not an attorney and this isn't intended as legal advice on copyrights. Do your own research.*)

EXPRESSIVE WRITING: A FOUNDATION FOR BUSINESS SUCCESS

Ronni Miller
Sarasota Branch
writeitout.com

You don't have to be a writer to express yourself through the medium of expressive writing.

I began writing in childhood. It was a way for me, a shy child, to express my views, insights, upsets and imagined thoughts. It was a way to vent. As a child, I had no idea about these grownup words like *vent* or even *express thoughts*. It was just a way for me to get my voice out of my head and down on paper. It made me feel happy to release it.

In 1999, I discovered that what I had been doing all my life had a name. It is called *expressive writing*. I first read about the term and its value in medicine when reading the research work of James W. Pennebaker, PhD. His research proved that writing about trauma reduced the effects of illnesses. Pennebaker and other scientific researchers in the field have documented the success of writing about trauma as it relates to wellness and reduces anxiety. I began to incorporate that concept into Write It Out ®, a program I created and taught to children and adults that began seven years earlier as a motivational program. For the last eighteen years it has segued into the health care field, where I facilitate expressive writing workshops at cancer centers and hospitals as well as in universities and education centers. It has become an important arm of my business, Write It Out.

How then can expressive writing, which I define as any writing in any genre that includes journal writing, poetry, prose and theater pieces, be a tool for creative artists in business?

Expressive writing:

- clears the cobwebs
- restarts the engine
- reduces anxiety
- taps into feelings, memories and experiences
- boosts health and well being
- recharges self-confidence and self-esteem
- fosters courage in the face of naysayers
- provides a venting outlet
- supports the vision

Most artists work alone, and the business side of creativity is often daunting. Many prefer to just create and have someone else, a magic genius, take over the business of selling, marketing and finances. All too often the artist, marketer, seller and financial person need to be all-in-one. This can cause stress and conflict.

Recently I spoke to an artist and illustrator who told me that, due to a letter she wrote to a client expressing enjoyment of painting a picture of the woman's grandchildren and inviting her to the studio to see more of her work, she was commissioned to do six paintings of characters from *The Wizard of Oz*. "This client is now a major collector of my work," said Karizu-Becher.

Another fine artist described how recording a dream in her journal led to an oil painting that won first prize in a juried show.

Take a few minutes to express your feelings and thoughts in writing or to record your dreams. You may find yourself just documenting or you may discover the pleasure of creating a poem or prose piece based on angst and thoughts. In either case, you will have used a simple method to release anxiety and help your business succeed.

The National League of American Pen Women, Inc., (NLAPW) is a group of professional women writers, artists and composers organized in 1897 in Washington, D.C., by female writers seeking to combat the inequality with which professionals of "the fair sex" were treated by their male counterparts. Our members are journalists, painters, choreographers, sculptors, illustrators, poets and songwriters, just to mention a few of the creative fields we encompass.

NLAPW is the oldest women's arts organization in the United States. More than 55,000 writers, artists and musicians have been proud to call themselves Pen Women. We currently have over 1,450 members and 73 branches.

Throughout NLAPW's 120-year history, members have illustrated how important the contribution of women's voices, minds and hands are to the arts. Grandma Moses and Georgia O'Keefe were famous Pen Women, as were Vinnie Ream, Eudora Welty, Pearl S. Buck, Eleanor Roosevelt, Amy Beach, Carrie Jacobs Bond, Mary McCleod Bethune and Maya Angelou.

NLAPW headquarters is the historic Pen Arts Building and Art Museum in Washington, D.C. The museum displays work by women artists in permanent and temporary exhibits and houses a library archiving the creative works of NLAPW members. It is also a home away from home for traveling members.

The Mission of NLAPW, a not-for-profit corporation, is to encourage, recognize and promote the production of creative work of professional standard in Art, Letters and Music and, through outreach activities, provide educational, professional and creative support to members and non-members in these disciplines. The core values of NLAPW are respect, knowledge, creation and preservation of the arts.

Learn more about NLAPW, Inc., by visiting www.NLAPW.org.

About the Editor:

Kathleen Powers-Vermaelen, M.F.A., has had work published in several literary magazines and anthologies. Her nonfiction book, *Publicize This! Promoting Your Group or Nonprofit on a Limited or Nonexistent Budget*, was published in 2014. An NLAPW Member-at-Large, she teaches literature and writing at Suffolk County Community College on Long Island.